A Stack of Napkins

1989-2014

A collection of bar and drink musings

Michael P. "Martini Mike" D'Arco

ISBN: 0692399852
ISBN-13: 978-0692399859 (House of D'Arco)

To all the people that have inspired, delighted, and encouraged me.

CONTENTS

Twenty five years of mixing business and pleasure come together in this delightful compilation of bar napkin scribblings, and post drink reminiscing. Though much can be considered poetry, some may have been more of notes to myself! Some have dates, some don't. Some I remember like it was yesterday, some I don't remember at all. Some locations are obvious from the bar's name printed on the napkin. Some others we will never know. But I do know I lived. I had a lot of good times along the way. And I interacted with a lot of interesting characters. I am happy to share this ride with you through my writing and photography. I dedicate this book to all the hospitality industry staffs and all my drinking buddies over the years. Cheers!

-Michael P. "Martini Mike" D'Arco

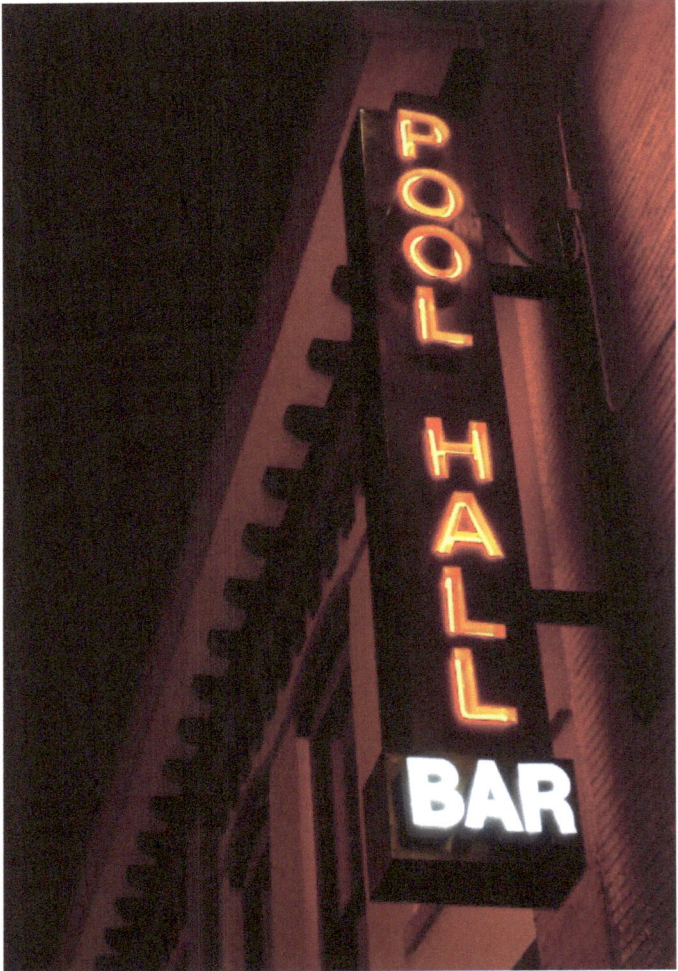

I Wonder

I wonder
      If they can see
          through
my thick walls
my brick walls.

Bricks
Soaked in Gin
Mortar
Soaked in Whisky

The rambling
   Brick Layers-
like the old fart
      planted to my right
      sucking down
    cool, working man's suds.
      Spitting up meanings
Known only to himself.

I wonder.

Ode to The Bow
(Rainbow Bar and Grill- Hollywood, CA)

We've been slithering about this den
since 1972.
Boas at the Bow
Kindred spirits
Brothers in arms
Allies
Three drinks away
from a memory together.
Lifelong friends made
over pizza, booze, and rock music.

Same guys,
different decade
Staff and customer alike,
including me.
Black leather
Anything's possible
Where's that pot o' gold?
Party favors?
Always good to see you

Past the big fireplace
Nod to the front booth
Survey the room
Don't look "them" in the eye
Head to the stairs

Upstairs
Late night and
Out of town guests
Instigate random pass throughs
 "The Lair"
Dark and cozy
Ripped from a pirate ship
Disheveled by the best
The elbows we have rubbed here
Watch your neck

The bathrooms have not changed as long as I have been coming here
They are the only undecorated space in the joint
Unless you count decals of unknown bands
And buckets of ice dumped into urinals
The only tales to tell here
Are between the mirrorless wall
And the cramped stall

Pick a stairway
Head back down
Never drinkless
Drink coupons or cash
Peruse the patio
Lemmy perched in his stool
Kick ass boots
Fielding annoying tourists with their phone cameras
He is cordial
We nod

Short skirts
Pre-gig band bites
Smoking
Joking
Winks and waves
Drinks and Daves

Producer Dave and I exchange tales of David Lee Roth
"You know Sonny Bones?"
Michael Des Barres walks by
No Ron Jeremy tonight
Rachael tells the tale of record producer Andy Johns tantrum that
ended with his scarf stuck in a 2" tape machine
We laugh
People you recognize from TV stand beside us.
We drink a little more than we should
A pizza smells and sounds good

 "If these booths could talk"
"I used to blow Led Zeppelin right where you're sitting"
OK, not exactly in those words
From the booth next door
The warm red arms of my booth hold me close
The faces on the wall monitor my response
John Belushi ate his last meal here
Marilyn Monroe and Joe DiMaggio had their first date here
Indeed, if these booths could talk

The "Bow"
The Rainbow
Home to ghosts of stars
Dead and alive
That I've met
Or wish I've met
Home to a cast of characters
Night after night after night
And here I am
Guess I didn't live quite fast enough
This is home
This will always be home
We are all family here
Check please.

Frolic Room
(Frolic Room- Hollywood, CA 1980s)

Put your money in the jukebox.
There's a dozen other people's money in there.
You'll have to wait.
Listen intently.

You'll have to drink.
Drink slowly.
Drink more.

What do you hear?
A ghostly silence?
NO
The other lonely fingers
dropping lonely coins
Together in a box
Together in a bar

Frolic absently
Fulfill the night
Grab the sight

Get your entertainment for your dollar
Whisper loud!
Wrestle, holler!

My song drifts out.
I drift...

Bourbon and Starlight

A spark
A tiny little spark
Even if only in my imagination
And the floodgates were opened.
Like the old days
Broke and depressed
Like now,
Again.

Words
Flowing
Like her healthy pour
Of bourbon and starlight
to drink in and savor.

Molecules
(Viper Room- Hollywood, CA 1990s)

Exiting souls
Entwined in chaos.
Peace
A drink away.
Infinity
A molecule away.

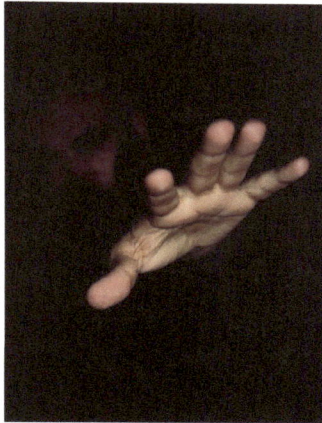

Finger .45
(Boardner's- Hollywood, CA 1980s)

She pulled her .45
"You better drink!"
Who was I to argue?
I guzzled
That wicked brew
Slow & cold
Hard & deep
Telling myself
The world spins free tonight.

Ashtray

They sat
Together
Lonely
Smoldering
in anxiety
Pitiful
in pleasure
One by one
Their names became undecipherable
Only charred remnants remained
Whisps of smoke
Flakes of ash
Taken deep.

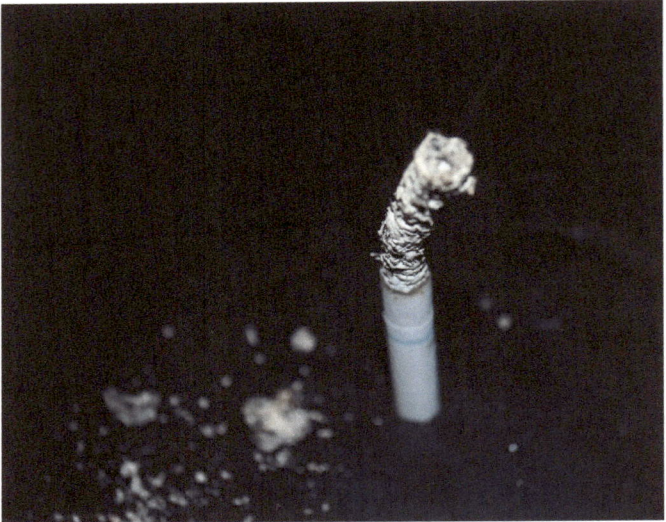

I'm a Sinner
(Zinc Cellar Bar- Albuquerque, NM)

Make me a Martini
You with your Scottish braids
With your healing smile
With your perfect ass

Discussion of bible study
Penetrates my ears from behind
I'm a sinner
in my heart,
in my mind.
Sin with me.

Fuel

As I pour in
the fuel
the fire begins
And I cannot stop it
Burning up my mind and soul

The devil dances
Deep inside
With madness or genius
I ponder
Over another cigarette and bourbon.

Untitled 7/1/10

The seemingly sad
broken
girls
linger and trudge
through the bar,
through the view,
almost smiling.
In need
of a kind word.

The Beautiful Ones
(1993)
Well who do you think gets the beautiful ones?
Somebody's got to.
The odds are that even a few might want me
A few not lost forever
In a haze
          of mistaken love
In a craze
  Starfuckers
Or worse...
In a daze
  over some rich, old, asshole

Like I'll be some day.

Float
(Monte Vista Fire Station – Albuquerque, NM 7/10/11)

She floated
through a side door
of the bar
and my brain.

My peripheral vision
focusing slowly,
delightfully.

Awakening my senses
she stood
like a vision
like my muse.

China Bar
(Flushing, NY)

New Wave called
It said "I'm over"
Followed by "WTF"
"What The Fuck", actually
As there were no cell phones during New Wave
Well, maybe there were.
But there was no texting.

And the bad Karaoke drones on.
The strange drinking games,
with dominos,
tempt me.

I am the only non-Asian present
I am the only post-college aged person present

They drink their weird cocktails
I slam tequila
Beer back

And at 4 am
We are all just people
Drunk
Happy
Friends

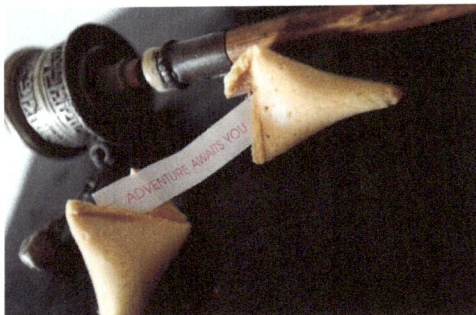

Love Talk

I listen
To the love talk
The relation talk
The strange, complicated ramblings
Of the things that
Could
Should
Would be…

Muse

Muse
Sing
Speak
Endless
Mysterious
Forever
Lost
Found
Muse

Uptown Drunks

Please Sir,
Stoli...
    with a twist
To numb the pain
From my clenched fist

I'd like
Just one
    Martini straight
I tell you
That's a drink I hate

I mingle with
The uptown drunks
Who so dislike
The downtown punks

Beer, bourbon
    Peanuts too
        That's a manly lunch for you

Uptown drunks
Don't think
    But think they think

    While I just grin and drink!

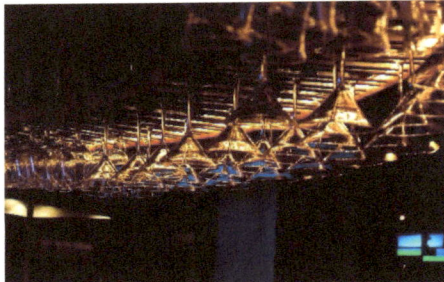

The Warm Center
(Little Joe's- Chicago, IL)

You know those places
that you're just drawn to?
This is one of those places

The last stand
Of a once thriving
Cultural center
This is practically all that is left
Of Little Italy

The ancient neon sign pulled me in
Like a damn firefly
Sinatra croons softly over my drink
Little Joe shuffles about

There's food available
From down the street
Unless of course it's Sunday
The old men drift in and out
Jubilantly discussing this week's gravy

There is tradition in this place
There is respect in this place
There are no whores in this place

I am overdressed
I am under drunk
I am firmly planted
At the end of this warm, worn bar

And as the locals file in
I am embraced
And I am the last gangster
Here, in the warm center

Vanishing Act

I do my best work
    Enclosed
In the bottle
    Hidden
From view
    of myself.

Mysterious, darkened eyes
    Tunneling
Down to the soul
    Repressed and exhilarated
        Free as a bird
            A crow.
    Gliding
        Diving
To the vanishing point.

Three Red Candles
(Boardner's- Hollywood, CA 1980s)

Three red candles
Light my way
And the shattered light
Invades my sight
Glowing up
Into our vast landscape
In the void of stools
At the mouth of Boardner's

And this signal
We know well
Speaking of the day
Gone
And the night
Sneaking in on her haunches

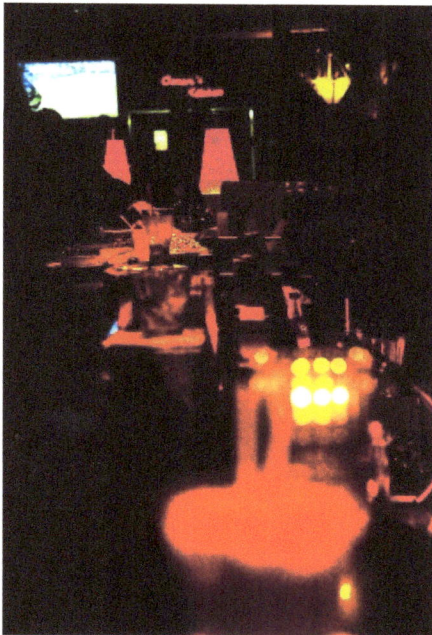

Stevie B's
(Boardner's- Hollywood, CA 1980s)

She had coffee eyes
Brazilian
Coffee eyes
Echoing life
Dark and sweet
Hollow yet full
Blinking in the candlelight
On the edge of forever
At Stevie B's

Honey lips
Speaking light
Killer talk
Poison and unforgettable
Kissing the world
Kissing my ears.

Reflections
(Los Angeles, CA late 1980's)

The upside down
Red neon
Blinking ominously
Off the top of the bar

The reflections noted
In my trance
My pupils fixed
      On the beacons
           Signaling out
Inviting my pain
And thrilling my abandon

Whisky

Sometimes I think
It's the vilest
Taste
But mostly I like it

Sweet as honey
Bites like a rattlesnake

When the fangs are in
There's not much use in shakin'

Abyss

The infinite desolation
Of the reality ritual
grips my very soul,
   and takes me
      further
         into
            The abyss...

Spin me Right Down
(Hotel Monteleone, Carousel Bar – New Orleans, LA)

Wow! I made it back to my hotel!
"Nawlens"?
"New Orleans"?
More drinks.

This is a bad bad idea
I see now
The bar actually spins
Oh God
Help me

It has been one long
Fuel filled
Day

From Green Chartreuse
In pirate lairs
To Rum
In jazz filled parks
And now pre-dinner Martinis
On a carousel

I need not your help
As the room spins
Or bar spins
Or my head spins

And then it's 2 am
On my back
Hungry
Fully clothed
Every light in the room on

I think I missed dinner.

Piece Man

Sitting
    Drinking
        Writing
Things
for other books

Finding
    my peace
Wishing
I could find a piece.

Tequila Nights

The mattress
thrown down
in the middle of the floor
cruised
like a great air ship
on a violet strip of sky.
With glittering walls
Of space
all around.
And I made shapeless
hand shadows
on my leg.
Those glorious nights.

A Toast

"A toast!", I said
"Everything's a poem you see"
"To jams, and toasts, and poetry!"
We chuckled
And drank
And jammed
And toasted some more
And wrote
And vanished

Anti-Social

Anti-social
Anti-social
Anti-social.
And their heads
Swayed
And bobbled
And laughed
of the unobvious
And asked, silently
for more beer

Untitled

Feeling a little crazy now
Like yesterday's dreams
are bouncing
Round and round
In a chaotic haze
    Of rubberized shit

26

Dangerous Drink

"Dangerous drink",
I commented.
He tipped his
dangerous cap.
The clock spinned.
My head spinned.
We continued the festivities.
And I dropped my liver.

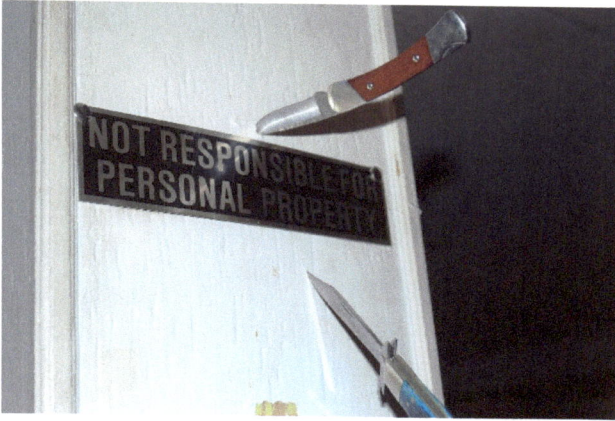

Solace

I find my solace in the bar
Where I hold back my darkness
Sometimes
For a few short moments
Only to relieve the pressure
Of the ordinary, everyday
Life
On my brain
Closing up the openings
On my imagination.

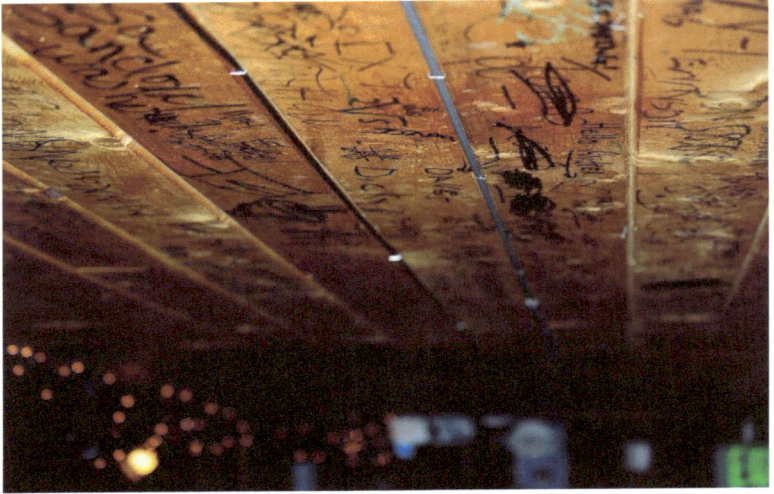

Joe's Place
(Joe's Place- Albuquerque, NM)

Down at Joe's
     The beer runs in rivers
          To my soul

Down the street
     And through the alley
          To my watering hole

And when I drink
     I drink my fill
          Enough to fly home
To my window sill

Numb

Numb enough
to think –
I don't care.
And maybe I don't.
About the people
About the pain
About the snow
Surrounding my streets
       that lead to
the bed, where
       I'll sleep alone
tonight.

Naked Beer

I wipe the sleep from my eyes
Only to find-
     I'm awake
Drifting into my world

It sure has changed
     I don't see
Any same
Any more

     Time ticking
          Not trusting
          Not knowing
          Not caring
          Drinking
               A beer
Naked

When only yesterday
I was cloaked in lies.

Bahama-rama

Oh indeed I need a pair
Of your delicious
Sugary
Rum filled
Coconuts

And an umbrella
And a straw

One for me
One for me

I chuckle at what she missed
Even keel
Take a picture
Turn up the music

I wince at the thought
Of sleeping alone
Tonight
On that damned cruise ship

The ocean breeze distracts me
So does the large breasted
Mannequin
I spy across the street

Anita

Anita-
    Where's your #?
Not callous
    or careless-
Just drunk
    and stupid.
And in search of
my perfect redhead.

So...
    What's your story?
Everybody has a story.

Are you lonely?
    All alone?
Left alone?
Someone left you alone?
Are you all alone?
Alone?

Minutes for Me

I drink in the minutes
Run from the clock
Ticking in the sky
Screaming in my mind

It's following me
Those hands
    As large as the moon

I don't see
I don't look
But, I know it's there
Counting and watching

Time ain't nothin' man
And I run faster
    Because that's what I do

My organs hit notes
Hypnotic and frightening
    Dragging me on
Infatuated with life

Carrying a song
That grows fresh
With each passing bar

Off beat and endless
Insane and holy
    Baptized
        in wine.

"The last thing I wanna do is 'jigger' everyone"!
– Whit, bartender

Medicine Park
(Medicine Park, OK)

This time machine
Is fueled by whisky

I am suddenly in the 1930's
On vacation
Here for the "healing";
Ladies
Booze
Card games
Cigars

The other gangsters and I
Drove all the way from Chicago
Cigars and Fedoras
Flasks and Tommy guns
Spit shines and pebbles

And the warm afternoon sun
Reminds us of when we were kids
Playing on the streets

And we stroll down to the water
And we tip our hats
And we think about tonight

Even gangsters need vacations
Even gangsters need fun

Free as the Breeze

I love the way
you wiggle
when you play pinball.

I love the way
your eyes light up
when you talk about something you're passionate about.

I love the way
you hug me so tight
 when you say goodbye.

I love the way
you collect little messages
from the spirits.

I love the way
you drink beer
like a man.

I love the way
you don't care what you wear.
Because, you are only out to impress yourself.

Maybe- I love the way
you disappear.
Because I anxiously await your return.

Bartender

Bartender
Nurse of the broken.
Talisman of hope.
Splendor and light
in a tunnel of darkness.
5 cent therapist.
Friend, confidante
 fantasy.
A sweet breathe of
faith and compassion
for the hopeless.
XO

36

Last Call
(Los Angeles, CA late 1980's)

Her sun drenched eyes
Silently blank
Unfocused
Behind the fire of the bar's edge
A familiar relief
Fell with her hair
And the exceeding repose
Of the final call
Echoed
Dominant
In our ears

Another Bar Napkin

Soiled in the night
       Lost
Like a thousand wishes
Like long since crumpled up dreams
And a million gallons of forgetfulness
Never to be retrieved...
    by the common man.

www.ingramcontent.com/pod-product-compliance
Lightning Source LLC
Chambersburg PA
CBHW040345060426
42445CB00029B/7